GRAPH RAG FOR
REAL WORLD

Solving Complex Problems with
Connected Data

OLIVER LUCAS JR

PREFACE

In today's data-driven world, the ability to extract meaningful insights from vast amounts of information is more critical than ever. Large Language Models (LLMs) have emerged as powerful tools for understanding and generating human-like text, but their reliance on pre-trained knowledge can limit their accuracy, context awareness, and scope, often leading to inaccuracies or "hallucinations." This book introduces Graph Retrieval Augmented Generation (Graph RAG), a groundbreaking approach that overcomes these limitations by combining the strengths of LLMs with the structured knowledge and reasoning capabilities of graph databases. By grounding LLMs in rich, interconnected data, Graph RAG unlocks new possibilities for complex reasoning, accurate information retrieval, and the development of truly intelligent applications. This book provides a practical and comprehensive guide to building and implementing Graph RAG systems, covering everything from fundamental concepts and architectural considerations to advanced techniques, real-world applications across diverse sectors, and crucial ethical considerations. Whether you're a developer, data scientist, researcher, or simply someone interested in the cutting edge of AI, this book will equip you with the knowledge and tools you need to understand and harness the transformative power of Graph RAG.

TABLE OF CONTENTS

Chapter 1

Chapter 2

Chapter 4

Chapter 5

Chapter 6

Chapter 7

Chapter 8

Chapter 9

Chapter 10

Chapter 1

Introduction to Graph RAG

1.1 The Evolution of Search and AI

I. Early Days: The Dawn of Search

Manual Indexes: Before computers, libraries used card catalogs and indexes to organize information.[1] This was the earliest form of "search," relying on human classification.

Early Digital Search: In the mid-20th century, with the rise of computers, simple text-based search emerged. Think of searching within a document using "Ctrl+F."

Keyword-Based Search: The first search engines like Archie (1990) indexed files on FTP servers, relying on exact keyword matches.[2] This was a major step but limited in understanding context.

II. The Rise of the Web and Search Engines

The World Wide Web: The invention of the web in the early 1990s created an explosion of information, making search engines essential.

Early Web Search Engines: Yahoo! (1994) started as a directory, while AltaVista (1995) offered full-text indexing, allowing users to search within web pages.[3]

The Google Revolution: Google's PageRank algorithm (1998) revolutionized search by analyzing the links between web pages, prioritizing more authoritative and relevant results.[4]

III. The Impact of AI on Search

Natural Language Processing (NLP): AI techniques like NLP enabled search engines to understand the meaning behind words and phrases, moving beyond simple keyword matching.[5]

Machine Learning (ML): ML algorithms allowed search engines to learn from user behavior, improving the relevance and personalization of search results.[6]

Semantic Search: This approach focuses on understanding the user's intent and the context of their query, providing more accurate and comprehensive results.[7]

IV. The Emergence of Graph-Based Search

Knowledge Graphs: Google's Knowledge Graph (2012) introduced the concept of representing information as interconnected entities and relationships, enabling a deeper understanding of the world.[8]

Graph Databases: Specialized databases designed to store and query graph data became increasingly important for efficient graph-based search.

The Limitations of Traditional Search: Despite advancements, traditional search methods still struggle with complex queries that require reasoning and combining information from multiple sources.

V. The Convergence: Graph RAG

Retrieval Augmented Generation (RAG): This approach combines the power of large language models (LLMs) with external knowledge sources to generate more informative and accurate responses.[9]

Graph RAG: The Next Step: By using knowledge graphs as the external knowledge source, Graph RAG enables more efficient and accurate retrieval of relevant information, leading to more intelligent and context-aware AI systems.[10]

1.2 What is Graph RAG and Why Does it Matter?

What is Graph RAG?

Building on RAG: To understand Graph RAG, we first need to understand Retrieval Augmented Generation (RAG). RAG is a technique that enhances Large Language Models (LLMs) by allowing them to access external knowledge sources. This helps LLMs overcome their limitations, such as:

Hallucinations: LLMs sometimes generate incorrect or nonsensical information.

Limited Knowledge: LLMs are trained on vast amounts of data, but their knowledge is still limited to what they were trained on.

Lack of Context: LLMs may struggle with questions that require specific context or knowledge not present in their training data.

Adding the "Graph": Graph RAG takes RAG a step further by using a **knowledge graph** as the external knowledge source. A knowledge graph is a way of representing information as a network of interconnected entities (nodes) and their relationships (edges).

How it Works: In a Graph RAG system:

A user asks a question.

The system uses the knowledge graph to retrieve relevant information related to the question. This retrieval process can involve complex graph traversals and semantic search.

The retrieved information is then provided as context to an LLM.

The LLM uses this context to generate a more accurate, relevant, and comprehensive answer.

Why Does it Matter?

Enhanced Accuracy and Reliability: By grounding LLMs in structured knowledge, Graph RAG reduces hallucinations and improves the factual accuracy of generated responses.

Deeper Understanding and Reasoning: Knowledge graphs capture complex relationships between entities, enabling LLMs to perform multi-hop reasoning and answer more complex questions.

Improved Contextual Awareness: Graph RAG provides LLMs with rich contextual information, allowing them to better understand the user's intent and provide more relevant responses.

Increased Transparency and Explainability: Because the retrieval process is based on a structured graph, it's easier to understand why a particular answer was generated, increasing transparency and trust in the system

Ability to Handle Complex Queries: Graph RAG excels at answering questions that require combining information from multiple sources or reasoning over complex relationships.

In essence, Graph RAG combines the strengths of:

Knowledge Graphs: Providing structured, interconnected knowledge.

Large Language Models: Enabling natural language understanding and generation.

This combination allows for the creation of more intelligent, reliable, and context-aware AI systems that can solve complex problems in various domains.

1.3 Key Concepts and Terminology

I. Core Graph Concepts:

Node (Vertex): Represents an entity, concept, or object. Examples: "Albert Einstein," "Theory of Relativity," "Princeton University."

Edge (Relationship/Link): Represents a connection or relationship between two nodes. Examples: "Albert Einstein *worked at* Princeton University," "Theory of Relativity *explains* gravity."

Graph: A collection of nodes and edges.

Directed Graph: Edges have a direction (e.g., "A *influences* B" is different from "B *influences* A")

Undirected Graph: Edges have no direction (e.g., "A *is related to* B" is the same as "B *is related to* A").

Property Graph: Nodes and edges can have properties (key-value pairs) that provide additional information. For example, the node "Albert Einstein" could have properties like "birthdate," "nationality," etc.

Graph Database: A database specifically designed for storing and querying graph data. Examples include Neo4j, Amazon Neptune, and JanusGraph.

II. Knowledge Graph Specific Terms:

Ontology/Schema: A formal representation of knowledge within a specific domain, defining the types of entities and relationships that can exist.

Triple: A basic unit of information in a knowledge graph, consisting of two nodes and the edge connecting them (Subject-Predicate-Object). Example: "Albert Einstein - born in - Ulm."

RDF (Resource Description Framework): A standard model for data interchange on the Web, often used for representing knowledge graphs.

SPARQL: A query language specifically designed for querying RDF data and knowledge graphs.

III. RAG Specific Terms:

Retrieval: The process of finding relevant information from the knowledge graph based on a user's query.

Retrieval Method: The specific algorithm or technique used for retrieval (e.g., graph traversal, semantic search, keyword search).

Context: The retrieved information that is provided to the LLM.

Generation: The process by which the LLM uses the context to generate a response.

Prompt: The input given to the LLM, including the user's query and the retrieved context.

Prompt Engineering: The process of designing effective prompts to elicit desired responses from LLMs.

IV. Graph RAG Specific Terms:

Graph Traversal: Exploring the graph by following edges from one node to another to find related information.

Semantic Search in Graphs: Using techniques like embeddings to find nodes and edges that are semantically similar to the user's query.

Multi-Hop Reasoning: Traversing multiple edges in the graph to infer new information or answer complex questions that require combining information from multiple sources.

Knowledge Graph Embedding: Representing nodes and edges as vectors in a high-dimensional space to capture semantic relationships.

By clearly defining these key terms, you'll ensure that your readers have a solid foundation for understanding the more complex concepts and techniques you'll discuss later in the book. It might be helpful to include a glossary at the end of the book as well for quick reference.

Chapter 2

Understanding Knowledge Graphs

2.1 Representing Knowledge as Graphs

1. The Basic Building Blocks: Nodes and Edges

Nodes (Entities): In a knowledge graph, nodes represent real-world entities, concepts, or objects. These can be concrete things like "Albert Einstein," "Paris," or "The Mona Lisa," or abstract concepts like "Relativity," "Love," or "Democracy."

Edges (Relationships): Edges define the relationships or connections between these nodes. They describe how the entities are related to each other. For example, "Albert Einstein *was born in* Ulm," "Paris *is the capital of* France," "The Mona Lisa *was painted by* Leonardo da Vinci."

2. Representing Knowledge with Triples

Subject-Predicate-Object: The most common way to represent knowledge in a graph is using triples. A triple consists of:

Subject: The starting node (e.g., "Albert Einstein").

Predicate: The relationship or edge (e.g., "was born in").

Object: The ending node (e.g., "Ulm").

Example: The statement "Albert Einstein was born in Ulm" is represented as the triple: (Albert Einstein, was born in, Ulm).

3. Types of Relationships

Knowledge graphs can represent various types of relationships:

Categorical: "A *is a* B" (e.g., "Dog *is a* Mammal")

Instance-of: "A *is an instance of* B" (e.g., "Snoopy *is an instance of* Dog")

Property-of: "A *has property* B" (e.g., "Apple *has property* Color")

Location: "A *is located in* B" (e.g., "Eiffel Tower *is located in* Paris")

Temporal: "A *occurred before* B" (e.g., "World War I *occurred before* World War II")

4. Properties on Nodes and Edges

Node Properties: You can add properties to nodes to provide more information about them. For example, the node "Albert Einstein" could have properties like "birthdate," "death date," "nationality," etc.

Edge Properties: Similarly, edges can have properties to provide more context about the relationship. For example, the edge "worked at" could have a property like "start date" or "end date."

5. Visualizing Knowledge Graphs

Knowledge graphs are often visualized as diagrams where nodes are represented as circles or boxes, and edges are represented as lines connecting them. This visual representation makes it easier to understand the relationships between different entities.

6. Benefits of Representing Knowledge as Graphs

Captures Complex Relationships: Graphs can represent intricate connections between entities, which is difficult to achieve with traditional relational databases.

Enables Reasoning and Inference: By traversing the graph, you can infer new knowledge or answer complex questions that require combining information from multiple sources.

Facilitates Data Integration: Knowledge graphs can integrate data from various sources into a unified representation.

Improves Search and Discovery: Graph-based search allows for more accurate and relevant results compared to keyword-based search.

2.2 Different Types of Knowledge Graphs

1. Based on Data Source and Construction:

Explicit Knowledge Graphs: These are built from structured data sources like databases, ontologies, and curated knowledge bases. They are often manually created or heavily curated by experts.

Examples: WordNet (lexical database), DBpedia (extracted from Wikipedia), Wikidata (collaboratively edited knowledge base).

Characteristics: High accuracy and consistency, well-defined schema, good for knowledge representation and reasoning.

Implicit Knowledge Graphs: These are constructed automatically from unstructured data sources like text, web pages, and social media. They rely on techniques like natural language processing (NLP) and information extraction.

Examples: Google Knowledge Graph (partially built from web data), knowledge graphs extracted from scientific literature.

Characteristics: Large-scale and comprehensive, capture a wide range of information, but may have lower accuracy and consistency compared to explicit knowledge graphs.

Hybrid Knowledge Graphs: These combine both explicit and implicit approaches, leveraging the strengths of each. They may start with an explicit knowledge base and then enrich it with information extracted from unstructured data.

2. Based on Scope and Domain:

General-Purpose Knowledge Graphs: These aim to capture general knowledge about the world, covering a broad range of topics and domains.

Examples: Google Knowledge Graph, DBpedia, Wikidata.

Characteristics: Wide coverage, suitable for general-purpose search and question answering.

Domain-Specific Knowledge Graphs: These focus on a specific domain or industry, such as healthcare, finance, or manufacturing.

Examples: Knowledge graphs for drug discovery, financial risk assessment, or supply chain management.

Characteristics: Deep and detailed knowledge within the specific domain, suitable for specialized applications and expert systems.

3. Based on Structure and Representation:

RDF (Resource Description Framework) Graphs: These use the RDF standard to represent knowledge as triples (Subject-Predicate-Object). They are often used for representing explicit knowledge graphs and are compatible with SPARQL query language.

Property Graphs: These allow nodes and edges to have properties (key-value pairs), providing more flexibility and expressiveness. They are commonly used in graph databases like Neo4j.

Labeled Property Graphs: A type of property graph where both nodes and relationships have labels, providing more semantic information.

4. Based on Purpose and Application:

Search Engine Knowledge Graphs: Used to enhance search results by providing contextual information and enabling semantic search.

Recommendation System Knowledge Graphs: Used to understand user preferences and recommend relevant items or content.

Question Answering Knowledge Graphs: Used to answer complex questions by retrieving and combining information from the graph.

Data Integration Knowledge Graphs: Used to integrate data from various sources into a unified representation.

2.3 Building and Maintaining Knowledge Graphs

I. Defining the Purpose and Scope

Business Goals: Start by clearly defining the goals and objectives of your knowledge graph. What problems are you trying to solve? What questions do you want to answer?

Domain and Scope: Determine the specific domain or area of knowledge that the graph will cover. This will help you focus your efforts and select relevant data sources.

Target Audience: Consider who will be using the knowledge graph and what their needs are.

II. Data Acquisition and Integration

Identifying Data Sources: Identify relevant data sources, which can include:

Structured Data: Databases, spreadsheets, APIs.

Unstructured Data: Text documents, web pages, research papers.

Existing Knowledge Bases: Publicly available knowledge graphs like DBpedia or Wikidata.

Data Extraction: Extract the necessary information from these sources using techniques like:

Database Queries: For structured data.

Web Scraping: For web pages

Natural Language Processing (NLP): For unstructured text.

Data Transformation: Transform the extracted data into a suitable format for the knowledge graph, such as RDF triples or property graphs.

Data Integration: Integrate data from different sources into a unified knowledge graph, resolving any inconsistencies or conflicts.

III. Knowledge Graph Modeling

Defining the Schema (Ontology): Create a schema or ontology that defines the types of entities and relationships that will be represented in the graph. This ensures consistency and facilitates reasoning.

Creating Nodes and Edges: Create nodes for the entities and edges for the relationships, populating the graph with data

Adding Properties: Add properties to nodes and edges to provide additional information and context.

IV. Technology Stack

Graph Database: Choose a suitable graph database to store and manage the knowledge graph. Options include:

Neo4j: A popular native graph database.

Amazon Neptune: A fully managed graph database service.

JanusGraph: An open-source, distributed graph database.

Tools and Libraries: Utilize tools and libraries for data extraction, transformation, and graph manipulation, such as:

Apache Jena: For working with RDF data.

RDFlib: A Python library for working with RDF.

GraphQL: A query language for APIs that can be used to access graph data.

V. Knowledge Graph Maintenance

Data Updates: Regularly update the knowledge graph with new information from various sources.

Data Quality: Implement processes to ensure data quality and consistency, such as data validation and cleaning.

Schema Evolution: Adapt the schema as needed to accommodate new types of entities and relationships.

Monitoring and Evaluation: Monitor the performance of the knowledge graph and evaluate its effectiveness in achieving its objectives.

VI. Key Considerations

Scalability: Design the knowledge graph to handle large amounts of data and complex queries.

Performance: Optimize the graph for efficient retrieval and query performance.

Security: Implement appropriate security measures to protect the knowledge graph from unauthorized access.

By covering these aspects, you'll provide a practical guide for your readers on how to build and maintain effective knowledge graphs for use in Graph RAG systems.

Chapter 3

The Power of Retrieval Augmented Generation (RAG)

3.1 Enhancing LLMs with External Knowledge

I. The Limitations of Standalone LLMs

Knowledge Cut-off: LLMs are trained on a snapshot of data up to a certain point. They lack access to real-time information or knowledge acquired after their training period.

Hallucinations: LLMs can sometimes generate incorrect or nonsensical information, often confidently presented as fact. This is because they are trained to generate text that is statistically likely, not necessarily factually accurate.

Lack of Specific Knowledge: While LLMs are trained on massive datasets, they may lack specific knowledge about niche topics, internal company data, or rapidly evolving fields.

Inability to Reason Deeply: LLMs can struggle with complex questions that require reasoning over multiple pieces of information or drawing inferences.

II. The Power of External Knowledge

Access to Up-to-Date Information: External knowledge sources can provide LLMs with access to the latest information, ensuring that their responses are current and relevant.

Grounding in Facts: By grounding LLMs in factual data, external knowledge helps reduce hallucinations and improves the accuracy of generated responses.

Specialized Knowledge: External knowledge sources can provide LLMs with access to specialized knowledge in specific domains, enabling them to answer complex questions in those areas.

Enhanced Reasoning Abilities: By providing LLMs with structured knowledge, they can perform more complex reasoning and draw more accurate inferences.

III. Methods for Enhancing LLMs with External Knowledge

Fine-tuning: Training an LLM on a specific dataset to improve its performance on a particular task or domain. While this can improve knowledge, it's computationally expensive and doesn't provide access to real-time information.

Prompt Engineering: Carefully crafting prompts to guide the LLM's response. This can be effective but relies on the LLM's existing knowledge and doesn't provide access to new information

Retrieval Augmented Generation (RAG): This is the most relevant method for your book. RAG involves:

Retrieval: Retrieving relevant information from an external knowledge source based on the user's query.

Augmentation: Providing the retrieved information as context to the LLM.

Generation: The LLM uses this context to generate a more informed and accurate response.

IV. The Advantages of RAG

Keeps LLMs Up-to-Date: RAG allows LLMs to access the latest information without requiring retraining.

Reduces Hallucinations: By grounding LLMs in factual data, RAG improves the accuracy and reliability of their responses.

Enables Specialized Knowledge: RAG can provide LLMs with access to specialized knowledge in any domain.

Improves Explainability: By showing the source of the information, RAG makes it easier to understand why an LLM generated a particular response.

V. Connecting to Graph RAG

This chapter sets the stage for explaining why *Graph* RAG is particularly powerful. You can emphasize how knowledge graphs, with their structured and interconnected nature, are an ideal external knowledge source for RAG, enabling more efficient retrieval, deeper reasoning, and improved context.

3.2 The RAG Pipeline: Retrieval, Generation, and Contextualization

This chapter is crucial for explaining the mechanics of RAG. Here's a breakdown of the RAG pipeline, focusing on retrieval, generation, and contextualization:

I. The RAG Pipeline Overview

The RAG pipeline typically consists of three main stages:

Retrieval: Identifying and retrieving relevant information from an external knowledge source based on the user's query.

Contextualization: Processing and formatting the retrieved information into a suitable context for the LLM.

Generation: Using the provided context, the LLM generates a response to the user's query.

II. Retrieval Stage

Query Understanding: The first step is to understand the user's query. This may involve techniques like:

Keyword Extraction: Identifying the most important keywords in the query.

Semantic Analysis: Understanding the meaning and intent behind the query.

Knowledge Source Selection: Choosing the appropriate knowledge source to retrieve information from. This could be a database, a document repository, a knowledge graph, or a combination of sources.

Retrieval Methods: Different techniques can be used for retrieval, depending on the type of knowledge source:

Keyword Search: Searching for documents or data that contain specific keywords.

Vector Search/Semantic Search: Using embeddings to find documents or data that are semantically similar to the query.

Graph Traversal (for Graph RAG): Exploring the graph by following edges from one node to another to find related information.

Ranking and Filtering: Ranking the retrieved information based on relevance and filtering out irrelevant results.

III. Contextualization Stage

Context Formatting: Formatting the retrieved information into a format that the LLM can understand. This may involve:

Text Formatting: Converting data into plain text.

Prompt Engineering: Creating a prompt that includes the retrieved information and the user's query.

Context Window Management: LLMs have a limited context window, which is the amount of text they can process at once. It's important to manage this window effectively by:

Truncation: Removing less relevant parts of the retrieved information.

Summarization: Condensing the retrieved information into a shorter summary.

Re-ranking or selection of only the most relevant passages.

Contextualization Techniques: Techniques to enhance the context provided to the LLM:

Adding Metadata: Including metadata about the retrieved information, such as source, date, or author.

Highlighting Key Information: Emphasizing the most important parts of the retrieved information.

IV. Generation Stage

LLM Input: The formatted context and the user's query are provided as input to the LLM.

Response Generation: The LLM generates a response based on the provided context.

Post-processing: The generated response may be post-processed to improve its quality, such as:

Filtering out irrelevant information.

Correcting grammatical errors.

Ensuring factual accuracy.

V. The Importance of Contextualization

Understand the relevance of the retrieved information to the query.

Integrate the retrieved information into its response effectively.

Avoid generating contradictory or inconsistent information.

3.3 Benefits and Limitations of Standard RAG

I. Benefits of Standard RAG

Improved Accuracy and Factual Grounding: By retrieving information from external sources, RAG reduces the reliance on the LLM's pre-trained knowledge, which can be outdated or contain inaccuracies. This leads to more factual and reliable responses.

Access to Up-to-Date Information: RAG allows LLMs to access real-time or frequently updated information, overcoming the knowledge cut-off problem of standalone LLMs.

Domain Specialization: RAG can be tailored to specific domains by using relevant knowledge sources. This enables LLMs to answer complex questions in specialized fields.

Reduced Hallucinations: By grounding responses in retrieved evidence, RAG minimizes the likelihood of LLMs generating incorrect or nonsensical information.

Enhanced Explainability: RAG can provide citations or links to the retrieved sources, making it easier to understand why a particular response was generated and increasing transparency.

Cost-Effectiveness (Compared to Fine-tuning): RAG is generally less computationally expensive than fine-tuning an LLM on a large dataset. It allows for the use of smaller, more efficient LLMs while still achieving good performance.

II. Limitations of Standard RAG

Retrieval Bottleneck: The performance of RAG is heavily dependent on the quality of the retrieval process. If irrelevant or insufficient information is retrieved, the LLM's response will be poor.

Context Window Limitations: LLMs have a limited context window, which restricts the amount of retrieved information that can be provided as context. This can lead to information loss or difficulty in handling complex queries that require a large amount of context.

Difficulty with Multi-Hop Reasoning: Standard RAG struggles with questions that require combining information from multiple sources or performing multi-step reasoning. It typically retrieves information in a single "hop," limiting its ability to answer complex queries requiring inference.

Challenges with Complex Queries: Queries that involve ambiguity, implicit information, or require deeper understanding of context can be difficult for standard RAG systems to handle effectively.

Data Format and Structure Dependence: Standard RAG often relies on unstructured or semi-structured data, which can be challenging to process and retrieve information from efficiently. It often relies on vector databases and semantic search, which has its own set of limitations, such as difficulty in capturing complex relationships.

Computational Cost of Retrieval: Retrieving relevant information from large datasets can be computationally expensive, especially for complex queries.

Lack of Contextual Understanding of Retrieved Information: Standard RAG may retrieve relevant text snippets but not fully understand the relationships between them. This can lead to the LLM generating responses that are factually correct but lack coherence or deeper understanding.

III. Setting the Stage for Graph RAG

This chapter should explicitly connect these limitations to the advantages offered by Graph RAG. For example:

Retrieval Bottleneck: Explain how knowledge graphs, with their structured nature and efficient graph traversal algorithms, can significantly improve retrieval accuracy and efficiency.

Difficulty with Multi-Hop Reasoning: Emphasize how graph traversal enables multi-hop reasoning, allowing Graph RAG to answer complex queries that require combining information from multiple sources.

Data Format and Structure Dependence: Highlight how knowledge graphs provide a structured and interconnected representation of knowledge, overcoming the limitations of unstructured data.

By clearly outlining the benefits and limitations of standard RAG, you create a compelling argument for the need for Graph RAG and prepare the reader for the subsequent chapters that delve into its specifics.

Chapter 4

Designing Your Graph RAG System

4.1 Defining Use Cases and Requirements

This is a vital step before diving into implementation details. Here's a breakdown of how to define use cases and requirements for a Graph RAG system:

I. Identifying Potential Use Cases

Start by brainstorming potential applications where Graph RAG could provide significant value. Look for scenarios that exhibit the following characteristics:

Complex Relationships: The domain involves intricate relationships between entities that are crucial for understanding and reasoning.

Need for Contextual Understanding: Questions or tasks require a deep understanding of context and the ability to connect disparate pieces of information.

Multi-Hop Reasoning: Answering questions often involves combining information from multiple sources or performing multi-step inferences.

Knowledge-Intensive Tasks: The application relies heavily on factual knowledge and domain expertise.

Here are some examples of potential use cases:

Customer Support: Providing accurate and comprehensive answers to complex customer inquiries by connecting product information, user manuals, and support tickets.

Drug Discovery: Identifying potential drug candidates by analyzing relationships between genes, diseases, and chemical compounds.

Financial Analysis: Assessing risk and identifying investment opportunities by analyzing relationships between companies, markets, and economic indicators.

Knowledge Management: Building intelligent knowledge bases that allow users to easily find and connect relevant information within an organization.

Legal Research: Assisting legal professionals in finding relevant precedents and case law by analyzing relationships between legal documents and court decisions.

II. Defining Specific Requirements

Once you have identified potential use cases, you need to define specific requirements for your Graph RAG system. These requirements should be based on the needs of the users and the specific tasks that the system will perform.

Here are some key aspects to consider:

Data Sources: Identify the relevant data sources that will be used to build the knowledge graph. Consider the format, quality, and accessibility of these sources.

Knowledge Graph Schema: Define the schema or ontology that will be used to represent the knowledge in the graph. This includes defining the types of entities and relationships that will be represented.

Query Types: Identify the types of questions or queries that the system will need to answer. Consider the complexity of these queries and the types of reasoning that will be required.

Retrieval Performance: Define the required retrieval performance, such as the speed and accuracy of retrieving relevant information from the graph.

LLM Selection: Choose an appropriate LLM based on its capabilities and performance characteristics.

Context Window Management: Determine how the context window of the LLM will be managed, considering the amount of retrieved information that needs to be provided as context.

Evaluation Metrics: Define the metrics that will be used to evaluate the performance of the Graph RAG system, such as accuracy, precision, recall, and F1-score.

III. Example: Customer Support Use Case

Let's take the customer support use case as an example. Here are some potential requirements:

Data Sources: Product catalogs, user manuals, support tickets, customer reviews.

Knowledge Graph Schema: Entities: Products, Customers, Issues, Solutions. Relationships: "Product *has* *issue*Issue," "Customer *reported* Issue," "Solution *resolves* Issue."

Query Types: "What are the common issues with product X?" "How do I fix issue Y?" "What is the warranty for product Z?"

Retrieval Performance: Retrieve relevant information within 1 second.

LLM Selection: A powerful LLM capable of generating natural language responses and handling complex queries

Context Window Management: Summarize long documents or prioritize the most relevant information to fit within the context window.

Evaluation Metrics: Accuracy of answers, customer satisfaction, resolution time.

By carefully defining use cases and requirements, you can ensure that your Graph RAG system is designed to meet the specific needs of your users and provide valuable solutions to real-world problems. This also provides a clear benchmark for measuring success during development and after deployment.

4.2 Choosing the Right Graph Database

I. Key Factors to Consider

Data Model:

Property Graph vs. RDF: Determine whether a property graph model (nodes and edges with properties) or an RDF model (triples) is more suitable for your data. Property graphs are often more flexible and easier to use for many applications.

Query Language:

Cypher: A popular query language for property graphs, known for its expressiveness and ease of use.

SPARQL: The standard query language for RDF data.

Gremlin: A graph traversal language that can be used with various graph databases.

Scalability:

Horizontal Scalability: The ability to distribute the database across multiple servers to handle large datasets and high query loads.

Vertical Scalability: The ability to increase the resources (CPU, memory, storage) of a single server.

Performance:

Query Performance: The speed at which queries can be executed.

Traversal Performance: The efficiency of traversing the graph to find related information.

Transactions and Consistency:

ACID Properties: Ensuring atomicity, consistency, isolation, and durability of transactions.

Integration with Other Tools:

LLM Integration: How easily the database can be integrated with your chosen LLM.

Data Integration Tools: Compatibility with tools for data extraction, transformation, and loading (ETL).

Deployment Options:

Cloud-Based: Managed services offered by cloud providers (e.g., Amazon Neptune, Azure Cosmos DB).

On-Premise: Installing and managing the database on your own servers.

Community and Support:

Community Support: The availability of online forums, documentation, and community resources.

Commercial Support: The availability of professional support from the database vendor.

Cost:

Licensing Costs: Costs associated with licensing the database software

Infrastructure Costs: Costs associated with hardware, cloud services, and maintenance.

II. Popular Graph Database Options

Neo4j:

A popular native graph database with a strong focus on property graphs.

Uses the Cypher query language.

Offers good performance for traversals and complex queries.

Has a large and active community.

Offers both community and enterprise editions.

Amazon Neptune:

A fully managed graph database service offered by AWS.

Supports both property graphs (using Gremlin) and RDF (using SPARQL).

Scalable and highly available.

Integrates well with other AWS services.

JanusGraph:

An open-source, distributed graph database.

Supports property graphs and uses the Gremlin traversal language.

Designed for large-scale graph analytics.

TigerGraph:

A high-performance graph database designed for complex analytics and real-time applications.

Uses its own query language called GSQL.

Known for its scalability and performance.

Azure Cosmos DB:

A multi-model database service offered by Microsoft Azure that includes graph database capabilities.

Supports property graphs and uses the Gremlin API.

Offers global distribution and high availability.

III. Recommendations for Graph RAG

For Graph RAG applications, consider the following:

Neo4j: A good choice for many applications due to its ease of use, strong community, and good performance.

Amazon Neptune: A good option if you are already using AWS and need a scalable and managed service.

Consider Vector Search Integration: Some graph databases (like Neo4j) are beginning to integrate vector search capabilities directly, which can be beneficial for hybrid approaches combining semantic and structural search.

IV. Evaluation and Testing

It's crucial to evaluate and test different graph databases with your specific data and use cases before making a final decision. Consider factors like query performance, data loading speed, and ease of integration with your LLM and other tools.

By carefully considering these factors and evaluating different options, you can choose the right graph database to power your Graph RAG system.

4.3 Selecting Appropriate LLMs

Choosing the right Large Language Model (LLM) is crucial for the success of your Graph RAG system. Different LLMs have different strengths and weaknesses, and the optimal choice will depend on your specific use case and requirements. Here's a breakdown of factors to consider and some popular LLM options:

I. Key Factors to Consider:

Task Specificity:

Question Answering: Some LLMs are specifically trained for question answering tasks and excel at providing concise and accurate answers.

Text Generation: Others are better at generating creative text formats, like stories or poems.

Code Generation: Some are specialized in generating code in various programming languages.

Context Window Size: The context window refers to the amount of text the LLM can process at once. A larger context window allows the LLM to consider more retrieved information, which is crucial for Graph RAG.

Reasoning Abilities: Some LLMs are better at reasoning and inference than others. This is important for tasks that require combining information from multiple sources or drawing conclusions.

Factual Accuracy: The tendency of an LLM to generate factually correct information. RAG helps with this, but some LLMs have stronger pre-training in this area.

Speed and Latency: The speed at which the LLM generates responses. This is important for real-time applications.

Cost: The cost of using the LLM, which can vary depending on the model size, usage volume, and API provider.

Availability and Access: How easily you can access and integrate the LLM into your system (e.g., via API, open-source models).

Fine-tuning Capabilities: Some LLMs allow for fine-tuning on custom datasets, which can improve their performance on specific tasks.

Bias and Safety: It's important to consider potential biases in the LLM's training data and implement safety measures to prevent the generation of harmful or offensive content.

II. Popular LLM Options (as of late 2023 - this field changes rapidly):

OpenAI Models (GPT-3.5, GPT-4):

Known for their strong performance on various NLP tasks, including text generation, question answering, and code generation.

GPT-4 has a larger context window and improved reasoning abilities compared to GPT-3.5.

Available through the OpenAI API.

Google PaLM 2:

A powerful LLM with strong performance in reasoning, coding, and multilingual tasks.

Powers Google's Bard chatbot.

Access is currently primarily through Google's own products and APIs.

Meta Llama 2:

Open-source LLMs that are available for research and commercial use.

Offer different model sizes to balance performance and computational cost.

Allow for fine-tuning on custom datasets.

Anthropic Claude:

Focuses on safety and helpfulness. Designed to be less likely to generate harmful or biased content.

Available through an API.

III. Recommendations for Graph RAG:

Large Context Window: Prioritize LLMs with larger context windows to accommodate the retrieved information from the knowledge graph.

Reasoning Abilities: Choose an LLM with strong reasoning abilities to effectively utilize the structured information provided by the graph.

Consider Cost and Latency: Balance performance requirements with cost and latency considerations.

Experiment and Evaluate: It's important to experiment with different LLMs and evaluate their performance on your specific use case and dataset.

IV. Example Use Case Considerations:

Complex Question Answering (e.g., Drug Discovery): Prioritize LLMs with strong reasoning abilities and a large context window, even if they are more expensive.

Customer Support Chatbot (with simpler queries): A smaller, faster, and less expensive LLM may be sufficient.

By carefully considering these factors and evaluating different options, you can select the most appropriate LLM for your Graph RAG system and ensure its effectiveness in addressing your specific needs. Keep in mind that the LLM landscape is constantly evolving, so staying up-to-date with the latest advancements is important.

Chapter 5

Implementing Graph Retrieval Strategies

5.1 Graph Traversal Algorithms for Retrieval

I. Basic Graph Traversal Concepts:

Goal: To systematically visit the nodes and edges of a graph, starting from a given node (or set of nodes).

Use in Graph RAG: Used to find relevant information in the knowledge graph based on a user's query.

II. Key Graph Traversal Algorithms:

Breadth-First Search (BFS):

How it works: Explores the graph layer by layer, starting from the source node and visiting all its neighbors before moving to the next level.

Use in Graph RAG: Useful for finding information that is directly related to the entities mentioned in the user's query. For example, finding all the products manufactured by a specific company.

Advantages: Finds the shortest path between two nodes**Disadvantages:** Can be memory-intensive for large graphs.

Depth-First Search (DFS):

How it works: Explores the graph by going as deep as possible along each branch before backtracking.

Use in Graph RAG: Useful for exploring deeper relationships and finding information that is indirectly related to the user's query. For example, finding all the research papers that cite a specific paper, and then finding all the papers that cite those papers.

Advantages: Less memory-intensive than BFS.

Disadvantages: May not find the shortest path between two nodes.

PageRank:

How it works: Assigns a numerical weight to each node in the graph, representing its importance or influence. It's based on the idea that more important nodes are linked to by more other nodes.

Use in Graph RAG: Useful for ranking retrieved information based on its importance or relevance. For example, prioritizing information from authoritative sources.

Advantages: Effective for identifying influential nodes.

Disadvantages: Can be computationally expensive for very large graphs.

Shortest Path Algorithms (Dijkstra's, A):

How they work: Find the shortest path between two nodes in the graph, considering the weights of the edges. Dijkstra's algorithm works for graphs with non-negative edge weights, while A* is a more efficient algorithm that uses heuristics to guide the search.

Use in Graph RAG: Useful for finding the most direct relationship between entities mentioned in the query, or for finding the most relevant path of reasoning.

Advantages: Finds the optimal path.

Disadvantages: Can be computationally expensive for large graphs, especially A* if the heuristic is poorly chosen.

Graph Embeddings (Node2Vec, GraphSAGE):

How they work: Learn vector representations (embeddings) of nodes in the graph, capturing their structural and semantic relationships.

Use in Graph RAG: Useful for semantic search in graphs, finding nodes that are semantically similar to the user's query. They can also be used to enhance other traversal algorithms.

Advantages: Efficient for finding semantically similar nodes.

Disadvantages: May not capture all the complex relationships in the graph.

III. Combining Traversal Algorithms:

In many cases, a combination of traversal algorithms is used to achieve the best results. For example, you might use BFS to find directly related entities and then use PageRank to rank the retrieved information.

IV. Optimizing Graph Traversal for RAG:

Indexing: Creating indexes on nodes and edges can significantly speed up graph traversal.

Caching: Caching frequently accessed information can reduce the number of graph traversals required.

Query Optimization: Carefully designing graph queries to minimize the number of nodes and edges that need to be visited.

V. Example in Graph RAG:

Imagine a query: "What diseases are treated by drugs manufactured by Pfizer?"

Start with the "Pfizer" node.

Use BFS to find all connected "Manufactures" edges and the associated "Drug" nodes

For each "Drug" node, use BFS again to find connected "Treats" edges and the associated "Disease" nodes.

Optionally use PageRank or embeddings to rank the retrieved "Disease" nodes based on relevance.

By explaining these algorithms and their application in Graph RAG, you empower your readers to understand the core mechanisms behind efficient knowledge retrieval.

5.2 Semantic Search and Embeddings in Graphs

This is a key chapter for bridging traditional graph traversal with modern AI techniques. Here's a breakdown of semantic search and embeddings in the context of graph databases and Graph RAG:

I. The Need for Semantic Search in Graphs

Limitations of Keyword-Based Search: Traditional keyword-based search in graphs relies on exact matches of node or edge labels. This approach fails to capture semantic similarity or understand the meaning behind the query.

Example: A keyword search for "heart attack" might not retrieve information about "myocardial infarction," even though they refer to the same condition

The Power of Semantics: Semantic search aims to understand the meaning and intent behind the query, allowing for more accurate and comprehensive results.

II. Embeddings: Representing Meaning as Vectors

What are Embeddings? Embeddings are vector representations of data (words, phrases, sentences, nodes, or even entire graphs) in a high-dimensional space. These vectors capture the semantic meaning of the data, such that semantically similar items are located closer together in the vector space.

How They Work: Embedding models are trained on large datasets to learn these vector representations. Different models use different architectures and training objectives, but the general idea is to capture the context and relationships between data points.

III. Types of Embeddings for Graphs:

Node Embeddings: Focus on representing individual nodes in the graph as vectors.

Node2Vec: Uses random walks to explore the graph and learn embeddings that capture the local neighborhood of each node.

DeepWalk: Similar to Node2Vec but uses truncated random walks.

GraphSAGE: Learns embeddings by aggregating information from the node's neighbors.

Edge Embeddings: Focus on representing the relationships between nodes as vectors.

Graph Embeddings: Represent entire graphs as vectors, capturing their overall structure and properties.

IV. Semantic Search in Graphs using Embeddings:

Embed the Query: Convert the user's query into an embedding vector using the same embedding model used to embed the graph data.

Embed the Graph Data: Generate embeddings for the nodes or edges in the graph.

Calculate Similarity: Calculate the similarity between the query embedding and the graph data embeddings using metrics like cosine similarity or Euclidean distance.

Retrieve Relevant Information: Retrieve the nodes or edges with the highest similarity scores.

V. Advantages of Using Embeddings in Graph RAG:

Captures Semantic Similarity: Allows for retrieving information that is semantically related to the query, even if there are no exact keyword matches.

Handles Complex Queries: Can handle queries that involve ambiguity or implicit information.

Improves Retrieval Accuracy: Can significantly improve the accuracy of retrieval compared to keyword-based search.

Enables Hybrid Approaches: Can be combined with traditional graph traversal algorithms to achieve even better results. For example, using embeddings to pre-filter candidate nodes before performing a more detailed graph traversal.

VI. Example in Graph RAG:

Imagine a knowledge graph about scientific publications and a query: "Find papers related to treatments for diabetes.

Embed the query "treatments for diabetes."

Embed the titles and abstracts of all papers in the graph.

Calculate the cosine similarity between the query embedding and the paper embeddings.

Retrieve the papers with the highest similarity scores, even if they don't contain the exact phrase "treatments for diabetes."

VII. Integrating with Graph Traversal:

Semantic search with embeddings can be used as a pre-filtering step before applying graph traversal algorithms. This allows you to narrow down the search space and improve the efficiency of traversal.

By explaining these concepts, you show how semantic search and embeddings enhance the retrieval capabilities of Graph RAG, enabling it to handle more complex and nuanced queries.

5.3 Optimizing Retrieval Performance

Optimizing retrieval performance is crucial for building a responsive and efficient Graph RAG system. Here's a breakdown of key optimization techniques:

I. Data Modeling and Schema Design:

Normalization: Properly normalize your data to avoid redundancy and improve query performance. For example, store common properties like dates or locations in separate nodes and link them to the relevant entities.

Indexing: Create indexes on frequently queried properties to speed up lookups. Most graph databases support indexing on node and edge properties.

Schema Optimization: Design your schema to reflect the most common query patterns. For example, if you frequently query for related entities based on a specific relationship type, ensure that this relationship is efficiently modeled.

II. Query Optimization:

Minimize Traversal Depth: Avoid unnecessary deep traversals of the graph. If possible, rewrite queries to find the required information with fewer hops.

Use Efficient Traversal Algorithms: Choose the appropriate traversal algorithm for the task. BFS is generally faster for finding directly connected entities, while DFS is more suitable for exploring deeper relationships.

Filtering Early: Apply filters as early as possible in the query to reduce the number of nodes and edges that need to be processed.

Avoid Cartesian Products: Be careful with queries that can result in large Cartesian products (combinations of all possible pairs of nodes). These queries can be very computationally expensive.

Parameterization: Use parameterized queries to avoid query parsing overhead and prevent SQL injection vulnerabilities (if applicable).

III. Caching:

Query Caching: Cache the results of frequently executed queries to avoid redundant computations.

Node/Edge Caching: Cache frequently accessed nodes and edges in memory to speed up retrieval.

IV. Graph Database Configuration and Tuning:

Memory Allocation: Allocate sufficient memory to the graph database to avoid disk I/O.

Storage Optimization: Use appropriate storage configurations and indexing strategies to optimize data access.

Connection Pooling: Use connection pooling to reduce the overhead of establishing database connections.

V. Hardware Considerations:

Sufficient Resources: Ensure that your hardware has sufficient CPU, memory, and storage to handle the graph size and query load

Fast Storage: Use fast storage devices like SSDs to reduce disk I/O latency.

Network Optimization: Optimize network connectivity between the application and the graph database.

VI. Embedding Optimization (for semantic search):

Efficient Similarity Search: Use efficient data structures and algorithms for similarity search, such as k-d trees, ball trees, or locality-sensitive hashing (LSH).

Approximate Nearest Neighbor (ANN) Search: Consider using ANN search algorithms for faster but approximate similarity search. These algorithms can significantly speed up retrieval with a small trade-off in accuracy.

Embedding Indexing: Create indexes on the embedding vectors to accelerate similarity search.

VII. Batching and Parallelization:

Batch Queries: Batch multiple queries together to reduce communication overhead between the application and the graph database.

Parallelize Retrieval: Parallelize graph traversals or similarity searches to utilize multiple CPU cores.

VIII. Monitoring and Profiling:

Monitoring Performance Metrics: Monitor key performance metrics such as query execution time, memory usage, and CPU utilization.

Profiling Queries: Use profiling tools to identify performance bottlenecks in specific queries.

IX. Example Optimizations:

Instead of: `MATCH (a)-[:RELATED_TO*]->(b) WHERE a.name = "X" RETURN b` (potentially very slow for deep traversals)

Try: `MATCH (a)-[:RELATED_TO]->(b) WHERE a.name = "X" RETURN b` (finds directly related entities only) or use indexing on `a.name`.

By implementing these optimization techniques, you can significantly improve the retrieval performance of your Graph RAG system and ensure that it can handle complex queries efficiently. Regular monitoring and profiling are key to identifying and addressing performance bottlenecks over time.

Chapter 6

Integrating with Language Models

6.1 Prompt Engineering for Graph-Augmented Prompts

I. Understanding the Goal of Graph-Augmented Prompts:

The primary goal is to provide the LLM with relevant information from the knowledge graph in a way that allows it to generate accurate, informative, and contextually appropriate responses. The prompt needs to:

Clearly state the user's query.

Present the retrieved graph data in a structured and understandable format.

Guide the LLM in how to use the graph data.

II. Key Components of a Graph-Augmented Prompt:

User Query: The original question or request from the user.

Retrieved Information (Context): Data extracted from the knowledge graph, including:

Nodes: Entities relevant to the query.

Edges: Relationships between those entities.

Properties: Attributes of the nodes and edges.

Instructions/Guidance: Explicit instructions to the LLM on how to use the provided context.

III. Prompt Engineering Techniques:

Structured Formatting: Present the retrieved graph data in a clear and structured format. Common approaches include:

Triples (Subject-Predicate-Object): Suitable for RDF graphs. Example: `(Albert Einstein, wasBornIn, Ulm)`

Key-Value Pairs: Suitable for property graphs. Example: `Node: Albert Einstein {birthdate: 1879, nationality: German}`

Tables or Lists: Can be used to present multiple related entities and their properties.

Explicit Instructions: Provide clear instructions to the LLM on how to use the context. Examples:

"Use the following information to answer the question."

"Based on the provided relationships, infer the answer."

"Consider the properties of the entities when generating your response.

Contextualization and Summarization: If the retrieved information is extensive, summarize it to fit within the LLM's context window. Focus on the most relevant aspects.

Few-Shot Learning (Optional): Include a few examples of how to use graph data to answer questions. This can help the LLM understand the desired output format and reasoning process.

Prompt Templates: Create reusable prompt templates for different types of queries. This can help ensure consistency and efficiency.

IV. Example Prompts:

Scenario: Knowledge graph about movies and actors.

User Query: "Who directed movies starring Leonardo DiCaprio and Kate Winslet?"

Retrieved Information:

Nodes: Leonardo DiCaprio, Kate Winslet, Titanic, Revolutionary Road, James Cameron, Sam Mendes

Edges: (Leonardo DiCaprio, starredIn, Titanic), (Kate Winslet, starredIn, Titanic), (Leonardo DiCaprio, starredIn, Revolutionary Road), (Kate Winslet, starredIn, Revolutionary Road), (James Cameron, directed, Titanic), (Sam Mendes, directed, Revolutionary Road)

Example Prompt (using Triples):

Question: Who directed movies starring Leonardo DiCaprio and Kate Winslet?

Context:
(Leonardo DiCaprio, starredIn, Titanic)
(Kate Winslet, starredIn, Titanic)
(James Cameron, directed, Titanic)
(Leonardo DiCaprio, starredIn, Revolutionary Road)
(Kate Winslet, starredIn, Revolutionary Road)
(Sam Mendes, directed, Revolutionary Road)

Answer:

Example Prompt (using Key-Value Pairs and Instructions):

Question: Who directed movies starring Leonardo DiCaprio and Kate Winslet?

Context:
Movie: Titanic {stars: [Leonardo DiCaprio, Kate Winslet], director: James Cameron}
Movie: Revolutionary Road {stars: [Leonardo DiCaprio, Kate Winslet], director: Sam Mendes}

Use the provided movie information to answer the question.

Answer:

V. Iterative Prompt Refinement:

Prompt engineering is an iterative process. Experiment with different prompt formats and instructions to find what works best for your specific use case and LLM.

VI. Considerations for Graph RAG:

Complexity of Graph Data: For more complex graph structures or multi-hop relationships, you may need to use more sophisticated prompt formatting techniques.

LLM Capabilities: Choose prompt formats that are well-suited to the capabilities of your chosen LLM.

By carefully engineering your prompts, you can maximize the effectiveness of your Graph RAG system and enable the LLM to generate high-quality responses based on the rich information contained in your knowledge graph.

6.2 Contextualizing Retrieved Information for LLMs

Contextualizing retrieved information is a critical step in the RAG pipeline, especially in Graph RAG. It's not enough to simply provide raw data; you need to present it to the LLM in a way that maximizes its understanding and ability to generate relevant and accurate responses. Here's a breakdown of key techniques:

I. The Importance of Contextualization:

Bridging the Gap: Contextualization bridges the gap between the structured data in the knowledge graph and the natural language understanding capabilities of the LLM.

Improving Relevance: It helps the LLM understand *why* the retrieved information is relevant to the user's query.

Enabling Reasoning: It facilitates the LLM's ability to reason over the retrieved information and draw inferences.

Reducing Hallucinations: By providing clear context, you ground the LLM's response in factual data, reducing the likelihood of generating inaccurate or fabricated information.

II. Contextualization Techniques:

Structured Formatting (as discussed in Prompt Engineering):

Triples (RDF): Clear and concise representation of relationships.

Key-Value Pairs (Property Graphs): Provides additional attributes for entities and relationships.

Lists and Tables: Useful for presenting multiple related entities or properties.

Adding Explanatory Text: Supplement the structured data with natural language explanations. This can help the LLM understand the context and significance of the retrieved information.

Example: Instead of just providing `(Albert Einstein, bornIn, Ulm)`, you could provide: "Albert Einstein was born in Ulm, Germany."

Highlighting Key Information: Emphasize the most relevant parts of the retrieved information. This can be done using bolding, italics, or other formatting techniques.

Summarization: Condense large amounts of retrieved information into concise summaries. This is especially important when dealing with LLMs with limited context windows.

Relationship Explanation: Explicitly explain the relationships between retrieved entities.

Example: Instead of just providing `(Company A, acquired, Company B)`, you could provide: "Company A acquired Company B, meaning that Company A now owns and controls Company B."

Temporal Context: If the knowledge graph contains temporal information (e.g., dates, time periods), provide this context to the LLM. This is crucial for understanding events that occurred in the past or for making predictions about the future.

Provenance and Source Information: Include information about the source of the retrieved data. This can help the LLM assess the reliability and credibility of the information.

Contextual Linking: If possible, link the retrieved information back to the original source in the knowledge graph. This allows the LLM to access more detailed information if needed.

III. Example of Contextualization:

User Query: "What are the symptoms of COVID-19?"

Retrieved Information (Raw):

Nodes: COVID-19, Fever, Cough, Fatigue, Shortness of breath

Edges: (COVID-19, hasSymptom, Fever), (COVID-19, hasSymptom, Cough), (COVID-19, hasSymptom, Fatigue), (COVID-19, hasSymptom, Shortness of breath)

Contextualized Information (for the LLM):

"COVID-19 is a respiratory illness. Common symptoms include:

Fever: An elevated body temperature.

Cough: A persistent or dry cough.

Fatigue: Feeling tired or lacking energy.

Shortness of breath: Difficulty breathing or feeling like you can't get enough air."

IV. Context Window Management and Prioritization:

Relevance Ranking: Prioritize the most relevant information for inclusion in the context.

Chunking and Summarization: Break down large amounts of information into smaller chunks and summarize each chunk.

Multi-Turn Interactions: If the context is too large to fit within a single prompt, consider using multi-turn interactions, where the LLM asks clarifying questions or requests additional information.

V. Graph RAG Specific Considerations:

Path Explanation: When retrieving information through graph traversals, explain the path that was taken. This can provide valuable context for the LLM.

Example: "To find the treatments for disease X, we traversed the graph from the 'Disease' node to the 'TreatedBy' edge and then to the 'Drug' node."

By effectively contextualizing the retrieved information, you can significantly improve the performance of your Graph RAG system and enable the LLM to generate more accurate, relevant, and insightful responses. This is a crucial step for unlocking the full potential of combining knowledge graphs and LLMs.

6.3 Fine-tuning LLMs for Graph RAG

Fine-tuning can significantly enhance the performance of LLMs specifically for Graph RAG tasks, but it's important to understand when and how to use it effectively. Here's a breakdown:

I. When to Consider Fine-tuning:

Domain Specialization: If your Graph RAG system is focused on a very specific domain (e.g., medical research, legal documents), fine-tuning can help the LLM better understand the specific terminology and relationships within that domain.

Performance Optimization: If you've optimized your retrieval and contextualization strategies but are still not achieving the desired performance, fine-tuning can be a powerful next step.

Specific Task Adaptation: If you have a very specific task in mind (e.g., generating summaries of research papers based on graph data), fine-tuning can help the LLM tailor its output to that task

Improved Reasoning on Graph Data: While prompt engineering can guide the LLM, fine-tuning can directly teach it to better understand and reason over structured graph data.

II. When Fine-tuning Might Not Be Necessary (or Ideal):

General-Purpose Applications: If your Graph RAG system needs to handle a wide range of queries across different domains, fine-tuning on a specific domain might not be beneficial and could even hurt performance on out-of-domain queries.

Rapidly Changing Knowledge: If the knowledge graph is constantly being updated with new information, frequent fine-tuning can become computationally expensive and impractical. RAG's strength is its ability to access changing information without retraining.

Limited Data: Fine-tuning requires a substantial amount of labeled training data. If you have limited data, fine-tuning might not be effective and could lead to overfitting.

Cost and Computational Resources: Fine-tuning large LLMs can be very expensive and require significant computational resources.

III. Data Preparation for Fine-tuning:

Creating a Training Dataset: The training dataset should consist of examples of user queries, retrieved graph data, and the desired LLM responses.

Data Format: The data should be formatted in a way that is suitable for the chosen LLM and fine-tuning framework. Common formats include JSON or text files with specific delimiters.

Example Data Point:

JSON

```
{
  "query": "What are the side effects of drug X?",
  "context": [
    "(Drug X, hasSideEffect, Nausea)",
    "(Drug X, hasSideEffect, Dizziness)"
  ],
    "response": "The side effects of drug X include nausea and
dizziness."
}
```

Data Augmentation: Consider augmenting your training data by generating variations of existing examples or creating synthetic data.

IV. Fine-tuning Process:

Choosing a Pre-trained Model: Select a pre-trained LLM that is suitable for your task and has sufficient capacity.

Selecting a Fine-tuning Framework: Choose a suitable fine-tuning framework, such as Hugging Face Transformers or other cloud-based solutions.

Setting Hyperparameters: Carefully tune the hyperparameters of the fine-tuning process, such as learning rate, batch size, and number of epochs.

Evaluation and Monitoring: Evaluate the performance of the fine-tuned model on a held-out test set and monitor its performance during training to prevent overfitting.

V. Fine-tuning Strategies for Graph RAG:

Focus on Graph Reasoning: Design training examples that require the LLM to reason over graph data, such as multi-hop reasoning or path finding.

Contextual Understanding: Create examples that emphasize the importance of context and require the LLM to integrate information from different parts of the graph.

Prompt Formatting Awareness: Train the LLM to be sensitive to the specific prompt formatting used in your Graph RAG system.

VI. Combining Fine-tuning with Prompt Engineering:

Fine-tuning and prompt engineering are complementary techniques. Even after fine-tuning, prompt engineering can still be used to further optimize the LLM's performance.

VII. Example Use Case:

A pharmaceutical company building a Graph RAG system for drug discovery could fine-tune an LLM on a dataset of drug-target interactions, side effects, and clinical trial data. This would allow the LLM to better understand the relationships between these entities and generate more accurate predictions about drug efficacy and safety.

By carefully considering these factors and using appropriate techniques, you can effectively fine-tune LLMs for Graph RAG tasks and achieve significant performance improvements. However, remember that fine-tuning is not always necessary and should be used strategically.

Chapter 7

Graph RAG in Action: Use Cases

7.1 Customer Support and Chatbots

This chapter should delve into the practical application of Graph RAG in customer support and chatbot development. Here's a structured approach:

I. The Challenges of Traditional Customer Support:

High Volume of Inquiries: Customer support teams often face a large volume of inquiries, leading to long wait times and customer frustration.

Repetitive Questions: Many customer inquiries are repetitive and can be easily answered with readily available information.

Difficulty Handling Complex Issues: Complex issues that require combining information from multiple sources can be challenging for human agents to handle efficiently.

Inconsistent Information: Providing consistent and accurate information across different support channels can be difficult.

II. How Graph RAG Can Improve Customer Support:

24/7 Availability: Graph RAG-powered chatbots can provide instant support 24 hours a day, 7 days a week.

Instant Answers to Common Questions: By leveraging a knowledge graph of product information, FAQs, and troubleshooting guides, chatbots can instantly answer common customer questions.

Efficient Handling of Complex Issues: Graph RAG can connect disparate pieces of information from various sources, enabling chatbots to handle complex issues that require multi-step reasoning.

Consistent and Accurate Information: By relying on a central knowledge graph, Graph RAG ensures that customers receive consistent and accurate information across all support channels.

Personalized Support: Graph RAG can personalize the support experience by considering customer history, product usage, and other relevant information.

Reduced Support Costs: By automating the handling of routine inquiries, Graph RAG can reduce the workload on human agents and lower support costs.

III. Building a Graph RAG-Powered Customer Support Chatbot:

Knowledge Graph Construction:

Data Sources: Product catalogs, user manuals, FAQs, troubleshooting guides, support tickets, customer reviews.

Schema Design: Define entities (e.g., Products, Features, Issues, Solutions, Customers) and relationships (e.g., "Product *hasFeature* Feature," "Product *hasIssue* Issue," "Solution *resolves* Issue").

Retrieval Strategies:

Keyword-based retrieval: For simple questions.

Semantic search using embeddings: For more complex questions that require understanding the meaning and intent.

Graph traversal: To connect related information and answer multi-part questions.

Prompt Engineering:

Design prompts that effectively present the retrieved information to the LLM.

Include clear instructions on how to use the information to answer the customer's question.

LLM Selection:

Choose an LLM that is suitable for conversational interactions and can generate natural language responses.

Chatbot Integration:

Integrate the Graph RAG system with a chatbot platform or framework.

Feedback and Training:

Collect feedback from users to improve the chatbot's performance.

Continuously update the knowledge graph with new information and refine the retrieval and prompt engineering strategies.

IV. Example Interaction:

Customer: "My coffee machine is leaking. What should I do?"

Graph RAG System:

Retrieves information from the knowledge graph about common leaks in the specific coffee machine model.

Retrieves troubleshooting steps and solutions.

Chatbot Response:

"I understand your coffee machine is leaking. Based on our information, this could be due to a faulty seal or a clogged filter. Here are some troubleshooting steps you can try:

Check the seal around the water tank.

Clean the filter.

If the problem persists, please contact our support team for further assistance."

V. Advantages of Graph RAG over Traditional Chatbots:

Deeper Understanding: Graph RAG can understand the relationships between different concepts, allowing it to handle more complex and nuanced questions.

Improved Accuracy: By grounding responses in factual data from the knowledge graph, Graph RAG reduces the risk of generating incorrect or misleading information.

Greater Flexibility: Graph RAG can easily adapt to changes in product information or support procedures by updating the knowledge graph.

By illustrating the application of Graph RAG in customer support with concrete examples and comparisons, this chapter effectively demonstrates its practical value.

7.2 Drug Discovery and Healthcare

This is a high-impact area where Graph RAG can make a real difference. Here's a breakdown of how it applies to drug discovery and healthcare:

I. Challenges in Drug Discovery and Healthcare:

Vast Amounts of Data: The fields of drug discovery and healthcare generate enormous amounts of data, including genomic data, clinical trial data, scientific literature, and patient records.

Complex Relationships: These data are interconnected in complex ways, with relationships between genes, proteins, diseases, drugs, and side effects.

Time-Consuming Research: Traditional drug discovery is a lengthy and expensive process, often taking many years and significant investment.

Knowledge Gaps: It can be difficult for researchers and healthcare professionals to stay up-to-date with the latest research and findings.

II. How Graph RAG Can Transform Drug Discovery and Healthcare:

Accelerating Drug Discovery:

Target Identification: Graph RAG can analyze relationships between genes and diseases to identify potential drug targets.

Drug Repurposing: It can identify existing drugs that could be repurposed for treating other diseases by analyzing drug-target interactions and disease similarities.

Predicting Drug Interactions: It can predict potential drug interactions and side effects by analyzing relationships between drugs and their effects on the body.

Improving Clinical Decision Support:

Personalized Treatment Recommendations: Graph RAG can provide personalized treatment recommendations based on patient history, genetic information, and the latest research findings.

Diagnosis Support: It can assist healthcare professionals in diagnosing complex conditions by connecting symptoms, medical history, and diagnostic test results.

Access to Latest Research: It can provide healthcare professionals with easy access to the latest research and clinical guidelines.

Enhancing Patient Care:

Patient Education: Graph RAG-powered chatbots can provide patients with accurate and personalized information about their conditions and treatment options.

Remote Monitoring: It can analyze data from wearable devices and electronic health records to provide remote monitoring and early detection of health issues.

III. Building a Graph RAG System for Drug Discovery:

Knowledge Graph Construction:

Data Sources: Public databases (e.g., DrugBank, Gene Ontology, PubMed), clinical trial data, electronic health records.

Schema Design: Define entities (e.g., Genes, Proteins, Diseases, Drugs, Side Effects, Clinical Trials) and relationships (e.g., "Gene *isAssociatedWith* Disease," "Drug *targets* Protein," "Drug *hasSideEffect* Side Effect").

Retrieval Strategies:

Semantic search using embeddings to find related concepts and information.

Graph traversal to identify pathways and relationships between entities.

Prompt Engineering:

Design prompts that allow researchers to ask complex questions about drug targets, mechanisms of action, and potential side effects.

LLM Selection:

Choose an LLM with strong reasoning abilities and a large context window.

Integration with Existing Tools:

Integrate the Graph RAG system with existing drug discovery tools and workflows.

IV. Example Interaction:

Researcher: "Find potential drug targets for Alzheimer's disease."

Graph RAG System:

Retrieves information about genes and proteins associated with Alzheimer's disease from the knowledge graph.

Identifies potential drug targets based on their role in the disease pathway.

System Response:

"Based on our analysis, APP, PSEN1, and PSEN2 are key genes associated with Alzheimer's disease. These genes encode proteins involved in the formation of amyloid plaques, a hallmark of the disease. Therefore, these proteins could be potential drug targets."

V. Ethical Considerations:

Data Privacy: Ensuring the privacy and security of patient data is crucial.

Bias in Data: Addressing potential biases in the data used to build the knowledge graph.

Transparency and Explainability: Providing clear explanations of how the system arrives at its conclusions.

By focusing on the specific applications and benefits of Graph RAG in drug discovery and healthcare, this chapter effectively demonstrates its transformative potential in these critical fields.

7.3 Financial Analysis and Risk Management

This chapter should explore the application of Graph RAG in the finance industry, focusing on analysis and risk management. Here's a structured approach:

I. Challenges in Financial Analysis and Risk Management:

Interconnectedness of Financial Data: Financial markets are highly interconnected, with complex relationships between companies, markets, economic indicators, and news events.

Data Silos: Financial data is often scattered across different sources and formats, making it difficult to get a holistic view.

Real-Time Data and Volatility: Financial markets are highly dynamic, with data changing constantly. Risk management requires access to real-time information and the ability to react quickly to market changes

Complex Regulations: The financial industry is subject to complex regulations, requiring sophisticated analysis and reporting capabilities.

II. How Graph RAG Can Transform Financial Analysis and Risk Management:

Enhanced Financial Analysis:

Relationship Discovery: Graph RAG can uncover hidden relationships between companies, industries, and markets, providing deeper insights into market trends and investment opportunities.

Sentiment Analysis: By analyzing news articles, social media data, and other textual sources, Graph RAG can gauge market sentiment and identify potential risks.

Predictive Analytics: By combining graph data with machine learning models, Graph RAG can improve the accuracy of financial forecasts and risk assessments.

Improved Risk Management:

Counterparty Risk Assessment: Graph RAG can analyze the network of relationships between financial institutions to assess counterparty risk and identify potential systemic risks.

Fraud Detection: It can detect fraudulent activities by identifying unusual patterns and anomalies in financial transactions.

Regulatory Compliance: It can help financial institutions comply with complex regulations by providing a clear and auditable record of their activities.

III. Building a Graph RAG System for Financial Analysis:

Knowledge Graph Construction:

Data Sources: Financial news articles, company filings, market data, economic indicators, social media data.

Schema Design: Define entities (e.g., Companies, Industries, Markets, Economic Indicators, News Events) and relationships (e.g., "Company *operatesIn* Industry," "Company *isListedOn* Market," "News Event *affects*Market").

Retrieval Strategies:

Semantic search using embeddings to find relevant news articles and financial reports.

Graph traversal to analyze relationships between companies and markets.

Prompt Engineering:

Design prompts that allow analysts to ask complex questions about market trends, investment opportunities, and risk factors.

LLM Selection:

Choose an LLM with strong reasoning abilities and the ability to handle numerical data.

Integration with Existing Systems:

Integrate the Graph RAG system with existing financial analysis tools and risk management systems.

IV. Example Interaction:

Financial Analyst: "What is the potential impact of rising interest rates on the technology sector?"

Graph RAG System:

Retrieves information about the relationship between interest rates and technology stocks.

Retrieves news articles and analyst reports discussing the potential impact.

System Response:

"Rising interest rates can negatively impact the technology sector by increasing borrowing costs for companies and reducing investor appetite for growth stocks. Analyst reports suggest that companies with high debt levels and future growth expectations are particularly vulnerable. However, companies with strong cash flow and established market positions may be less affected."

V. Specific Use Cases:

Algorithmic Trading: Using Graph RAG to identify trading opportunities based on real-time market data and news sentiment.

Portfolio Optimization: Using Graph RAG to construct diversified portfolios that minimize risk and maximize returns

Credit Risk Assessment: Using Graph RAG to assess the creditworthiness of borrowers by analyzing their financial history and connections to other entities.

By illustrating these specific applications and benefits, this chapter effectively demonstrates the value proposition of Graph RAG in the financial industry. It's also important to touch on the sensitivity of financial data and the need for robust security and privacy measures.

Chapter 8

Evaluating and Monitoring Graph RAG Systems

8.1 Metrics for Measuring Performance

I. General RAG Evaluation Metrics:

These metrics apply to any RAG system, regardless of whether it uses a graph database.

Accuracy: Measures how often the generated responses are factually correct and consistent with the retrieved information.[1]

Precision: Measures the proportion of retrieved information that is relevant to the query.

Recall: Measures the proportion of relevant information that is retrieved.

F1-Score: The harmonic mean of precision and recall, providing a balanced measure of retrieval effectiveness.[2]

Relevance: Measures how well the generated responses address the user's query. This can be assessed through human evaluation or using automated metrics like BLEU or ROUGE scores (though these are more suited for text summarization tasks and less so for fact retrieval).

Faithfulness: Measures how well the generated responses are grounded in the retrieved information, avoiding hallucinations or unsupported claims.[3]

Contextual Relevance: Measures how well the retrieved information is contextualized and integrated into the generated response.

Latency: Measures the time it takes for the system to generate a response.[4]

Throughput: Measures the number of queries the system can handle per unit of time.

II. Graph-Specific Metrics:

These metrics are specifically relevant for Graph RAG systems and assess the effectiveness of graph retrieval.

Graph Coverage: Measures the proportion of the relevant subgraph that is retrieved.[5]

Path Accuracy: Measures how accurately the retrieved paths in the graph reflect the relationships between the entities mentioned in the query.

Hop Count: Measures the number of hops (edges traversed) required to retrieve the relevant information. Lower hop counts generally indicate more efficient retrieval.

Node/Edge Relevance: Measures the relevance of the retrieved nodes and edges to the query.

Structural Similarity: Measures the similarity between the retrieved subgraph and the ideal subgraph that would answer the query completely.

III. Evaluation Methods:

Human Evaluation: Human evaluators assess the quality of the generated responses based on criteria like accuracy, relevance, fluency, and helpfulness. This is the most reliable method but can be expensive and time-consuming.

Automated Evaluation: Automated metrics like precision, recall, F1-score, BLEU, and ROUGE can be used to evaluate the performance of the system automatically. However, these metrics may not fully capture the nuances of human judgment.

A/B Testing: Comparing different versions of the Graph RAG system (e.g., with different retrieval strategies or prompt engineering techniques) using A/B testing to determine which performs better.

IV. Metrics for Specific Use Cases:

Customer Support: Customer satisfaction, resolution time, first contact resolution rate.

Drug Discovery: Accuracy of drug target predictions, number of potential drug candidates identified.

Financial Analysis: Accuracy of financial forecasts, ability to identify risk factors.

V. Example Evaluation Scenario:

Imagine evaluating a Graph RAG system designed to answer questions about movies and actors.

Query: "Who directed movies starring Leonardo DiCaprio and Kate Winslet?"

Ideal Answer: James Cameron (Titanic), Sam Mendes (Revolutionary Road)

Retrieved Information: The system retrieves information about Titanic and Revolutionary Road, along with their directors and actors.

Evaluation:

Accuracy: The system correctly identifies the directors.

Relevance: The retrieved information is highly relevant to the query.

Graph Coverage: The system retrieves the relevant part of the graph connecting actors and directors.

Hop Count: The retrieval involves two hops (actor to movie, movie to director).

VI. Importance of Combining Metrics:

It's important to use a combination of metrics to get a comprehensive understanding of the system's performance. No single metric can capture all aspects of quality and effectiveness.

By understanding and applying these metrics, you can effectively evaluate the performance of your Graph RAG system and identify areas for improvement. This allows for data-driven optimization and ensures that the system meets the desired performance goals.

8.2 Debugging and Troubleshooting

You're right, debugging and troubleshooting are crucial for any complex system. Here's a more complete breakdown of common issues and how to address them in Graph RAG:

I. Common Issues and Troubleshooting Strategies:

Retrieval Issues:

No Results Retrieved:

Check Query Formulation: Ensure the query is correctly formulated and matches the data in the knowledge graph. Pay attention to case sensitivity, spelling, and synonyms.

Verify Graph Connectivity: Check if the entities mentioned in the query are actually connected in the graph. Visualize the graph if possible.

Inspect Indexing: Verify that the necessary indexes are created and functioning correctly in the graph database.

Debug Retrieval Logic: Step through the retrieval code to identify any errors in the logic, such as incorrect traversal paths or filtering conditions.

Irrelevant Results Retrieved:

Refine Retrieval Strategy: Adjust the retrieval algorithm or parameters to improve relevance. For example, if using BFS, limit the traversal depth. If using semantic search, adjust similarity thresholds.

Improve Semantic Search: If using embeddings, retrain the embedding model on a more relevant dataset or use a different embedding model altogether.

Review Knowledge Graph Data: Check for inconsistencies, errors, or missing relationships in the knowledge graph data. Data quality is paramount.

Slow Retrieval Performance:

Optimize Queries: Rewrite queries to minimize traversal depth and avoid Cartesian products. Use appropriate indexing.

Optimize Graph Database Configuration: Tune memory allocation, caching, and storage configurations in the graph database.

Profile Queries: Use profiling tools provided by the graph database to identify performance bottlenecks.

Hardware Upgrade: If necessary, upgrade hardware resources (CPU, memory, storage).

Contextualization Issues:

Incorrectly Formatted Context: Check that the retrieved information is formatted correctly for the LLM. Ensure proper use of delimiters, formatting, and instructions.

Insufficient Context: If the LLM is not generating relevant responses, it might not be receiving enough context. Try retrieving more information or summarizing it more effectively.

Excessive Context (Exceeding Context Window): If the retrieved information exceeds the LLM's context window, truncate or summarize it to fit within the limits. Prioritize the most relevant information.

Lack of Contextual Clarity: Ensure that the relationships between retrieved entities are clearly explained to the LLM.

LLM Generation Issues:

Hallucinations: If the LLM is generating incorrect or nonsensical information, double-check the retrieved information and the prompt. Ensure that the context is clear and unambiguous.

Irrelevant Responses: If the LLM's responses are not relevant to the query, review the retrieval and contextualization steps. The LLM might be receiving irrelevant context.

Poorly Formatted Responses: If the LLM's responses are poorly formatted, adjust the prompt instructions to guide the LLM to generate responses in the desired format.

Bias in Responses: If the LLM's responses exhibit bias, review the training data used to train the LLM and the data in the knowledge graph for potential biases.

Integration Issues:

API Errors: Check for errors in the API calls to the graph database or the LLM.

Data Format Mismatches: Ensure that the data formats used by the different components of the system are compatible.

Network Connectivity Issues: Check for network connectivity problems between the different components of the system.

II. Debugging Tools and Techniques:

Logging: Implement comprehensive logging to track the flow of data and identify potential errors.

Debugging Tools: Use debugging tools provided by your programming language and development environment.

Graph Database Visualization: Use graph visualization tools to inspect the knowledge graph and verify the connections between entities.

Prompt Inspection: Carefully inspect the prompts being sent to the LLM to identify any formatting errors or inconsistencies.

Unit Testing: Write unit tests to verify the functionality of individual components of the system.

End-to-End Testing: Perform end-to-end testing to ensure that the entire system works correctly.

III. Example Debugging Scenario:

A user asks, "What are the side effects of aspirin?" The system retrieves information about aspirin but the LLM responds with information about ibuprofen.

Possible Cause: The knowledge graph might have an incorrect or missing relationship between aspirin and its side effects, or there might be an unintended connection between aspirin and ibuprofen.

Troubleshooting Steps:

Visualize the graph: Inspect the nodes for aspirin and ibuprofen and their connections to side effect nodes.

Check retrieval logic: Verify the query being sent to the graph database and ensure it's targeting the correct relationships.

Inspect retrieved data: Log the exact data retrieved from the graph and sent to the LLM.

By systematically applying these debugging and troubleshooting strategies, you can effectively identify and resolve issues in your Graph RAG system and ensure its reliability and performance.

8.3 Monitoring for Data Drift and Concept Drift

Monitoring for data drift and concept drift is crucial for maintaining the long-term performance and reliability of a Graph RAG system. These phenomena can significantly impact the accuracy and relevance of retrieved information and generated responses.

I. Understanding Data Drift and Concept Drift:

Data Drift: Refers to changes in the statistical properties of the input data over time. In a Graph RAG context, this could mean changes in the distribution of node properties, relationship types, or the overall structure of the graph.

Example: New products are added to a product catalog, changing the distribution of product categories.

Concept Drift: Refers to changes in the underlying relationships between data or the meaning of concepts over time. In a Graph RAG context, this could mean changes in the relationships between entities in the knowledge graph or changes in the way users formulate their queries.

Example: The meaning of a medical term changes due to new research findings, or customer preferences for product features shift.

II. Impact on Graph RAG:

Retrieval Inaccuracy: Data drift can lead to the retrieval of irrelevant or outdated information.

Reduced Response Relevance: Concept drift can cause the LLM to generate responses that are no longer relevant or accurate in the current context.

Increased Hallucinations: Both data drift and concept drift can increase the likelihood of the LLM generating hallucinations.

III. Monitoring Techniques:

Data Distribution Monitoring:

Track Statistical Properties: Monitor the statistical properties of node properties and edge attributes over time, such as mean, standard deviation, and frequency distributions.

Use Statistical Tests: Use statistical tests (e.g., Kolmogorov-Smirnov test, Chi-squared test) to detect significant changes in data distributions.

Graph Structure Monitoring:

Track Graph Metrics: Monitor graph metrics such as the number of nodes, edges, average degree, and diameter over time.

Detect Structural Changes: Use graph comparison algorithms to detect changes in the graph structure.

Query Monitoring:

Track Query Patterns: Monitor the types of queries being asked by users over time

Analyze Query Performance: Track metrics such as retrieval time and response relevance for different types of queries.

LLM Output Monitoring:

Monitor Response Quality: Regularly evaluate the quality of the LLM's responses using human evaluation or automated metrics

Detect Changes in Response Patterns: Look for changes in the topics, sentiment, or style of the LLM's responses.

IV. Detection Strategies:

Regular Data Audits: Periodically review the data in the knowledge graph for accuracy and completeness.

Anomaly Detection: Use anomaly detection techniques to identify unusual changes in data distributions or graph structure.

Feedback Loops: Implement feedback mechanisms to collect user feedback on the quality of the system's responses.

Version Control for Knowledge Graph: Use version control systems to track changes to the knowledge graph and revert to previous versions if necessary.

V. Mitigation Strategies:

Knowledge Graph Updates: Regularly update the knowledge graph with new information to reflect changes in the real world.

Schema Updates: Update the schema of the knowledge graph if necessary to accommodate new concepts or relationships.

Retraining Embedding Models: Retrain embedding models periodically to ensure that they capture the latest semantic relationships.

Prompt Engineering Adjustments: Adjust prompt engineering strategies to adapt to changes in user query patterns.

Fine-tuning LLM (If Necessary): If concept drift is significant and frequent, consider fine-tuning the LLM on updated data. However, as noted previously, this is a more resource-intensive approach.

Automated Retraining/Updating Pipelines: Ideally, establish automated processes for updating the knowledge graph, retraining embeddings, and even potentially triggering alerts for significant drift.

VI. Example Scenario:

A Graph RAG system is used for e-commerce product recommendations. Over time, new product categories become popular, and customer preferences shift.

Data Drift: The distribution of product categories in the knowledge graph changes.

Concept Drift: The relationships between products and customer preferences change.

Monitoring: The system detects a decrease in click-through rates and an increase in negative user feedback.

Mitigation: The knowledge graph is updated with new product categories and customer preference data. The embedding model is retrained, and prompt engineering strategies are adjusted.

By actively monitoring for data drift and concept drift and implementing appropriate mitigation strategies, you can ensure that your Graph RAG system remains accurate, relevant, and effective over time. This proactive approach is essential for maintaining a high-quality user experience and maximizing the value of your system.

Chapter 9

Advanced Graph RAG Techniques

9.1 Multi-Hop Reasoning and Inference

I. What is Multi-Hop Reasoning?

Single-Hop Reasoning: Involves retrieving information directly connected to the entities mentioned in the query. For example, "What is the capital of France?" requires a single hop from "France" to its "capital."

Multi-Hop Reasoning: Involves traversing multiple relationships (hops) in the graph to connect disparate pieces of information and infer new knowledge. For example, "What is the nationality of the artist who painted the Mona Lisa?" requires multiple hops: from "Mona Lisa" to its "artist" (Leonardo da Vinci), and then from "Leonardo da Vinci" to his "nationality."

II. How Graph RAG Enables Multi-Hop Reasoning:

Graph Traversal Algorithms: Graph RAG uses graph traversal algorithms (like BFS, DFS, or more specialized pathfinding algorithms) to explore the connections between entities in the knowledge graph.

Path Finding: Multi-hop reasoning essentially involves finding a path between two or more entities in the graph. The length of the path corresponds to the number of hops.

Combining Information from Multiple Sources: By traversing multiple relationships, Graph RAG can gather information from different parts of the knowledge graph and combine it to answer complex questions.

III. Examples of Multi-Hop Reasoning in Graph RAG:

Example 1: Drug Discovery: "What diseases can be treated by drugs that target the EGFR protein?" This requires multiple hops: from "EGFR protein" to "drugs that target it," and then from those "drugs" to the "diseases they treat."

Example 2: Financial Analysis: "What is the impact of a change in oil prices on companies in the airline industry?" This involves multiple hops: from "oil prices" to "industries affected by oil prices," and then filtering for companies in the "airline industry."

Example 3: Customer Support: "What accessories are compatible with the latest version of product X, and where can I buy them?" This requires multiple hops: from "product X" to its "compatible accessories," and then from those "accessories" to "retailers that sell them."

IV. Implementing Multi-Hop Reasoning in Graph RAG:

Query Decomposition: Complex queries can be decomposed into simpler sub-queries that can be executed independently. The results of these sub-queries can then be combined to answer the original query.

Path Ranking and Selection: When multiple paths exist between entities, ranking and selecting the most relevant path is crucial. This can be done using metrics like path length, edge weights, or node importance (e.g., PageRank).

Prompt Engineering for Multi-Hop Reasoning: The prompt provided to the LLM should clearly indicate the relationships between the retrieved entities and guide the LLM to perform the necessary inference.

Example Prompt: "Based on the following information: (A is related to B), (B is related to C), infer the relationship between A and C."

V. Challenges and Considerations:

Computational Complexity: Multi-hop reasoning can be computationally expensive, especially for large graphs with complex relationships.

Path Explosion: The number of possible paths between entities can grow exponentially with the number of hops, making it challenging to find the most relevant path.

Context Window Limitations: The retrieved information from multiple hops can easily exceed the LLM's context window. Effective summarization and prioritization techniques are crucial.

VI. Advanced Techniques:

Rule-Based Reasoning: Combining graph traversal with rule-based reasoning can enable more complex inferences.

Probabilistic Reasoning: Using probabilistic graph models to handle uncertainty and incomplete information.

Graph Neural Networks (GNNs): Using GNNs to learn representations of graph structures that capture multi-hop relationships.

By explaining multi-hop reasoning and providing concrete examples, this chapter will showcase one of the most significant advantages of using graph databases within a RAG architecture. It demonstrates how Graph RAG can go beyond simple fact retrieval and provide deeper insights by connecting disparate pieces of information.

9.2 Temporal Graph RAG

Temporal Graph RAG extends the capabilities of Graph RAG by explicitly considering the time dimension in the knowledge graph. This is crucial for applications where information changes over time, such as financial markets, social media, or medical records.

I. The Importance of Time in Knowledge Graphs:

Dynamic Relationships: Many relationships in the real world change over time. For example, a company might merge with another company, a person might change their job, or a disease might develop new symptoms.

Temporal Context: Understanding the time context of information is crucial for accurate reasoning and decision-making. For example, knowing when a drug was approved or when a research paper was published is essential for evaluating its relevance.

Event Sequencing: Many applications require understanding the sequence of events over time. For example, in medical records, it's important to know the order in which symptoms appeared or treatments were administered.

II. Representing Time in Knowledge Graphs:

Time-Stamped Nodes and Edges: The most common approach is to add timestamps or time intervals to nodes and edges. This can be done using properties or dedicated time-related data structures

Example: A "workedAt" edge between a person and a company could have properties like "startDate" and "endDate."

Temporal Nodes: Another approach is to create separate nodes to represent time points or time intervals. These nodes can then be connected to other entities using temporal relationships.

Example: A "PublicationEvent" node could be connected to a "ResearchPaper" node with a "publishedAt" edge.

Versioned Graphs: In some cases, it might be necessary to maintain multiple versions of the graph, each representing a snapshot of the knowledge at a specific point in time.

III. Temporal Graph Retrieval:

Temporal Queries: Queries can include temporal constraints to retrieve information relevant to a specific time period.

Example: "What were the most common side effects of drug X in 2022?"

Temporal Path Finding: Algorithms can be used to find paths in the graph that satisfy temporal constraints.

Example: "Find all events that occurred between 2020 and 2023 that are related to disease Y."

Temporal Embeddings: Embedding models can be extended to capture temporal information, allowing for semantic search in time-varying graphs.

IV. Temporal Contextualization for LLMs:

Time-Aware Prompts: Prompts should clearly indicate the time context of the retrieved information.

Example: "According to data from 2022, the most common side effects of drug X were..."

Event Sequencing in Context: When presenting information about a sequence of events, ensure that the order of events is clearly conveyed to the LLM

Temporal Reasoning Instructions: Provide explicit instructions to the LLM on how to reason about time

Example: "Consider the time order of events when generating your response."

V. Example in Temporal Graph RAG:

User Query: "How did the stock price of company A change after the announcement of its merger with company B in 2023?"

Temporal Graph RAG System:

Retrieves information about the merger event, including the date of the announcement.

Retrieves historical stock price data for company A before and after the announcement date.

System Response:

"Company A announced its merger with company B on [date in 2023]. Before the announcement, the stock price of company A was [price]. After the announcement, the stock price increased/decreased to [price], representing a change of [percentage]."

VI. Applications of Temporal Graph RAG:

Financial Time Series Analysis: Analyzing stock market trends, predicting financial risks, and detecting fraud.

Medical History Analysis: Tracking patient symptoms, diagnoses, and treatments over time.

Social Media Analysis: Analyzing trends in social media conversations and identifying events that trigger changes in sentiment.

Historical Research: Analyzing historical events and their relationships.

By incorporating temporal information into Graph RAG, you can create systems that are more accurate, relevant, and capable of handling complex real-world scenarios. This is a crucial advancement for applications that deal with dynamic and time-sensitive information.

9.3 Handling Uncertainty and Inconsistency in Knowledge Graphs

Handling uncertainty and inconsistency is a critical challenge in building and using knowledge graphs, especially in Graph RAG systems. Real-world data is often incomplete, ambiguous, or contradictory, and knowledge graphs need to be able to handle this effectively.

I. Sources of Uncertainty and Inconsistency:

Data Entry Errors: Mistakes made during data entry or extraction can lead to incorrect or inconsistent information.

Conflicting Information from Different Sources: Different sources might provide conflicting information about the same entity or relationship.

Incomplete Information: The knowledge graph might not contain all the relevant information about a particular topic.

Ambiguous Language: Natural language used to describe entities and relationships can be ambiguous or have multiple interpretations.

Evolving Knowledge: Knowledge changes over time, and information that was once true might become outdated or incorrect.

II. Representing Uncertainty in Knowledge Graphs:

Probabilistic Edges: Assign probabilities or confidence scores to edges to represent the likelihood that a relationship exists.

Example: `(John, hasDisease, Cancer, probability: 0.8)` indicates an 80% chance that John has cancer.

Fuzzy Logic: Use fuzzy logic to represent vague or imprecise concepts.

Provenance Information: Store information about the source of the data to assess its reliability

Contextual Information: Provide context about the conditions under which a statement is true.

III. Handling Inconsistency in Knowledge Graphs:

Conflict Resolution Strategies: Implement strategies to resolve conflicting information from different sources. This could involve prioritizing certain sources, using voting mechanisms, or manually reviewing the conflicting information.

Data Validation and Cleaning: Implement data validation rules and cleaning procedures to detect and correct errors in the data.

Versioning and Provenance Tracking: Track the history of changes to the knowledge graph to identify the source of inconsistencies.

IV. Impact on Graph RAG:

Retrieval of Uncertain or Inconsistent Information: The retrieval process needs to be able to handle uncertainty and retrieve information with associated probabilities or confidence scores.

LLM Handling of Uncertainty: The LLM needs to be able to understand and reason about uncertain information.

Generating Responses with Uncertainty: The LLM should be able to express uncertainty in its responses when appropriate.

V. Strategies for Handling Uncertainty in Graph RAG:

Retrieval with Confidence Scores: Retrieve information from the knowledge graph along with its associated confidence scores.

Prompt Engineering for Uncertainty: Explicitly inform the LLM about the uncertainty of the retrieved information.

Example: "The following information is uncertain, with a confidence score of 80%: (John, hasDisease, Cancer)."

LLM Output with Uncertainty: Encourage the LLM to express uncertainty in its responses using phrases like "It is likely that...", "It is possible that...", or "There is some evidence to suggest that...".

Probabilistic Reasoning with LLMs: Explore techniques for incorporating probabilistic reasoning directly into the LLM's processing.

Fact Verification and Source Citation: When possible, have the LLM cite the sources of information and indicate their reliability.

VI. Example in Graph RAG:

User Query: "Does John have cancer?"

Retrieved Information:

```
(John, hasDisease, Cancer, probability: 0.8)

(John, hasTestResult, Negative, source: Test A)

(John, hasTestResult, Positive, source: Test B)
```

System Response:

"There is some uncertainty about whether John has cancer. There is evidence suggesting he has cancer (with an 80% probability), but he has also received conflicting test results. Test A was negative, while Test B was positive. Further investigation is needed to determine a definitive diagnosis."

VII. Advanced Techniques:

Probabilistic Graph Databases: Use graph databases that explicitly support probabilistic data.

Bayesian Networks: Use Bayesian networks to model probabilistic relationships between entities.

By addressing uncertainty and inconsistency effectively, you can build more robust and reliable Graph RAG systems that can handle the complexities of real-world data. This is especially important in domains like healthcare and finance, where accuracy and reliability are paramount.

Chapter 10

The Future of Graph RAG

10.1 Emerging Trends and Research Directions

This chapter should look towards the future of Graph RAG, exploring current research and emerging trends that are shaping its development.

I. Hybrid Architectures:

Combining Symbolic and Neural Approaches: Integrating symbolic reasoning methods (like logic programming or rule-based systems) with neural methods (like LLMs and graph neural networks) to combine the strengths of both approaches. This could lead to more robust and explainable systems.

Integrating Vector Databases with Graph Databases: Combining the strengths of vector databases (for semantic search) and graph databases (for structural relationships) to create hybrid retrieval systems that can leverage both semantic and structural information. This is already starting to appear in some graph database products.

II. Enhanced Knowledge Graph Construction and Maintenance:

Automated Knowledge Graph Construction: Developing more sophisticated methods for automatically extracting information from unstructured data and building knowledge graphs.

Continuous Knowledge Graph Updates: Implementing systems that can automatically update the knowledge graph with new information from various sources in real-time.

Knowledge Graph Fusion: Developing methods for merging and integrating different knowledge graphs to create larger and more comprehensive knowledge bases.

Self-Supervised Learning for Knowledge Graphs: Using self-supervised learning techniques to learn representations of knowledge graphs without requiring large amounts of labeled data.

III. Advancements in Graph Retrieval:

More Efficient Graph Traversal Algorithms: Developing more efficient algorithms for traversing large and complex graphs.

Learning to Navigate Graphs: Using machine learning to learn optimal traversal strategies for different types of queries.

Personalized Graph Retrieval: Developing methods for personalizing graph retrieval based on user preferences and context.

IV. Improved Contextualization and Prompt Engineering:

Dynamic Contextualization: Developing methods for dynamically adapting the contextualization strategy based on the query and the retrieved information.

Automated Prompt Engineering: Using machine learning to automatically generate effective prompts for different types of queries.

Explainable Contextualization: Developing methods for explaining why certain information was chosen as context and how it relates to the query.

V. Enhanced LLM Integration:

LLMs that can Directly Interact with Graphs: Developing LLMs that can directly query and reason over graph data without requiring explicit contextualization. This is a very active area of research.

Multi-Modal Graph RAG: Combining graph data with other modalities, such as images, videos, or audio, to create more comprehensive and informative responses.

LLM-Augmented Graph Construction: Using LLMs to assist in the process of building and maintaining knowledge graphs, such as by identifying new entities and relationships from text.

VI. Applications in New Domains:

Scientific Discovery: Using Graph RAG to accelerate scientific research by connecting disparate pieces of information from scientific literature and experimental data.

Education and Learning: Building intelligent tutoring systems that can provide personalized learning experiences based on individual student needs and knowledge gaps.

Cultural Heritage: Using Graph RAG to connect and explore information about historical events, artifacts, and cultural figures.

VII. Ethical Considerations and Responsible Use:

Bias Mitigation: Developing methods for mitigating bias in knowledge graphs and LLMs.

Privacy Preservation: Ensuring the privacy and security of sensitive data used in Graph RAG systems.

Transparency and Explainability: Making Graph RAG systems more transparent and explainable to build trust and accountability.

Responsible AI Development: Adhering to ethical principles and guidelines for AI development.

10.2 The Impact of Graph RAG on AI and Society

This concluding chapter should explore the broader implications of Graph RAG, considering its potential impact on AI as a field and its wider societal effects.

I. Impact on AI as a Field:

Bridging the Gap Between Symbolic and Neural AI: Graph RAG represents a significant step towards bridging the gap between symbolic AI (which emphasizes structured knowledge and reasoning) and neural AI (which emphasizes learning from data).[1] By combining knowledge graphs with LLMs, Graph RAG leverages the strengths of both approaches.[2]

Improving Explainability and Trustworthiness: The ability to trace the reasoning process through the knowledge graph makes Graph RAG systems more explainable and trustworthy than traditional black-box neural networks.[3]This is crucial for building trust in AI systems, especially in high-stakes domains.

Enabling More Complex Reasoning and Inference: Graph RAG enables AI systems to perform more complex reasoning and inference tasks, going beyond simple pattern recognition and enabling them to answer more complex and nuanced questions.[4]

Democratizing Access to Knowledge: By making vast amounts of structured knowledge easily accessible through natural language interfaces, Graph RAG can democratize access to information and empower users to learn and discover new insights.[5]

Driving Innovation in NLP and Knowledge Representation: Graph RAG is driving innovation in both natural language processing and knowledge representation, leading to the development of new techniques and tools for building and using knowledge graphs and LLMs.

II. Societal Impact:

Improved Decision-Making: By providing access to more accurate and comprehensive information, Graph RAG can improve decision-making in various domains, such as healthcare, finance, and government.[6]

Enhanced Productivity and Efficiency: By automating knowledge-intensive tasks, Graph RAG can enhance productivity and efficiency in various industries.

New Opportunities for Learning and Education: Graph RAG can create new opportunities for learning and education by providing personalized learning experiences and access to vast amounts of educational resources.[7]

Transformation of Industries: Graph RAG has the potential to transform various industries by enabling new applications and services that were previously impossible.[8]

Potential Challenges and Risks:

Bias Amplification: If the knowledge graph or the LLM is biased, Graph RAG can amplify these biases, leading to unfair or discriminatory outcomes.

Misinformation and Manipulation: Graph RAG could be used to spread misinformation or manipulate public opinion if not used responsibly.

Job Displacement: The automation of knowledge-intensive tasks could lead to job displacement in certain industries.

Data Privacy and Security: The use of sensitive data in knowledge graphs raises concerns about data privacy and security.[9]

III. Responsible Development and Deployment:

Bias Mitigation Strategies: Implement strategies to mitigate bias in knowledge graphs and LLMs.

Transparency and Explainability: Design Graph RAG systems to be transparent and explainable.

Ethical Guidelines and Regulations: Develop ethical guidelines and regulations for the development and deployment of Graph RAG systems.

Public Awareness and Education: Educate the public about the capabilities and limitations of Graph RAG and promote responsible use.

IV. The Future Vision:

The chapter should conclude with a forward-looking perspective on the future of Graph RAG. This could include:

Ubiquitous Knowledge Access: Imagine a future where everyone has easy access to the world's knowledge through natural language interfaces powered by Graph RAG.

Intelligent Assistants: Imagine intelligent assistants that can understand complex questions, perform multi-step reasoning, and provide personalized recommendations based on vast amounts of structured knowledge.

AI-Driven Scientific Discovery: Imagine Graph RAG accelerating scientific discovery by connecting disparate pieces of information from scientific literature and experimental data.

By exploring these broader implications and emphasizing the importance of responsible development, this concluding chapter provides a comprehensive and impactful overview of Graph RAG and its potential to shape the future of AI and society.

10.3 Ethical Considerations and Responsible Use

This is a crucial chapter, especially given the potential impact of Graph RAG. It should address the ethical implications and promote responsible development and deployment.

I. Bias in Knowledge Graphs and LLMs:

Data Bias: Knowledge graphs are built from data, and if that data reflects existing societal biases, the knowledge graph will inherit those biases. This can lead to discriminatory or unfair outcomes when the Graph RAG system is used.

Example: A knowledge graph about occupations might over-represent men in STEM fields and women in caregiving roles, perpetuating gender stereotypes.

Algorithmic Bias: LLMs are trained on massive datasets, and if these datasets contain biases, the LLMs will learn and perpetuate those biases.

Example: An LLM might generate more positive descriptions of people from certain demographic groups and more negative descriptions of people from other groups.

Impact on Graph RAG: Biased knowledge graphs and LLMs can lead to biased retrieval of information and biased generation of responses, reinforcing existing inequalities.

II. Mitigation Strategies for Bias:

Data Auditing and Cleaning: Carefully audit the data used to build the knowledge graph for potential biases and implement cleaning procedures to correct them.

Diverse Data Sources: Use data from diverse sources to reduce the risk of bias from any single source.

Bias Detection Techniques: Use statistical and computational methods to detect bias in knowledge graphs and LLMs.

Bias Mitigation Algorithms: Implement algorithms to mitigate bias in retrieval and generation processes.

Regular Evaluation and Monitoring: Regularly evaluate the system for bias and monitor its performance on different demographic groups.

III. Privacy Concerns:

Sensitive Data in Knowledge Graphs: Knowledge graphs can contain sensitive personal information, such as medical records, financial data, or social media activity.

Data Security and Access Control: It's crucial to implement robust security measures and access control mechanisms to protect this sensitive data from unauthorized access.

Data Anonymization and De-identification: Consider anonymizing or de-identifying data before it is added to the knowledge graph.

Compliance with Privacy Regulations: Ensure that the system complies with relevant privacy regulations, such as GDPR and CCPA.

IV. Misinformation and Manipulation:

Potential for Misuse: Graph RAG could be used to spread misinformation or manipulate public opinion by providing false or misleading information.

Content Moderation and Fact-Checking: Implement content moderation and fact-checking mechanisms to prevent the spread of misinformation.

Source Transparency and Citation: Encourage the system to cite the sources of information and provide context about their reliability.

User Education and Awareness: Educate users about the potential for misinformation and how to critically evaluate information provided by Graph RAG systems.

V. Explainability and Transparency:

Understanding the Reasoning Process: It's important for users to understand how the system arrives at its conclusions.

Explainable AI (XAI) Techniques: Use XAI techniques to make the system's reasoning process more transparent and understandable.

Provenance Tracking: Track the sources of information and the steps involved in the retrieval and generation processes.

VI. Accountability and Responsibility:

Clear Lines of Responsibility: Establish clear lines of responsibility for the development, deployment, and use of Graph RAG systems

Ethical Guidelines and Frameworks: Adhere to established ethical guidelines and frameworks for AI development.

Stakeholder Engagement: Engage with stakeholders, including users, domain experts, and ethicists, to ensure that the system is developed and used responsibly.

VII. Responsible Deployment and Use:

Use Case Evaluation: Carefully evaluate the potential risks and benefits of using Graph RAG for specific use cases.

User Training and Education: Provide users with adequate training and education on how to use the system responsibly.

Continuous Monitoring and Improvement: Continuously monitor the system's performance and address any ethical concerns that arise.

VIII. Example Ethical Dilemma:

A Graph RAG system is used to assess credit risk. If the system is trained on biased data, it might unfairly deny loans to people from certain demographic groups.

Mitigation:

Carefully audit and clean the credit data to remove any biases.

Monitor the system's performance on different demographic groups and adjust the algorithms if necessary.

Provide clear explanations of how credit risk is assessed.

By thoroughly addressing these ethical considerations and promoting responsible use, you can help ensure that Graph RAG is used for beneficial purposes and avoids harmful consequences. This chapter should emphasize that ethical considerations are not an afterthought but an integral part of the entire development lifecycle.

www.ingramcontent.com/pod-product-compliance
Lightning Source LLC
Chambersburg PA
CBHW071006050326
40689CB00014B/3512